I0201126

Love is in My Mother, the Moon

Also by Kilaya Ciriello

THE SCORPIO RING OF FIRE:
AN ASTROLOGICAL JOURNEY INTO THE HEART OF THE
GALACTIC CENTER

THE BHAGAVAD GITA IN FOCUS:
A COMPILATION WITH COMMENTARY

Kilaya Ciriello

Love is in My Mother, the Moon

poems from Amritapuri, India

Tripureswari Books
Southampton, New York

First Tripureswari Book Edition, January 2017
Copyright © 2015 Kilaya Ciriello
ISBN: 978-0-9888015-4-7
Library of Congress Control No.: 2015903589
Printed by CreateSpace, an Amazon Company

This book is dedicated to that red round pulse of life.

The triple goddess.

TRIPURESWARI.

Who I can't deny no matter how much I try.

INTRODUCTION

I first arrived at Amritapuri, the sprawling ashram of the spiritual teacher/humanitarian leader Amma, located in the southern state of Kerala, India, in July of 2010. I arrived not knowing much about where I was. I had never thought of going to India before I started traveling with Amma through the U.S. that summer and so, I didn't have much in the way of expectations. My dreams for travel, prior to that, had mostly involved solitude and natural wild spaces which are two things India is not known for. Going to India that first time, all I had was my love for my guru.

Over the next three years I lived at Amritapuri, on and off, and these poems were written during those stays. I found something quite unexpected happening to me while in India and more specifically, while at the ashram. I fell in love in an unexpected way. In love with what? Most times I didn't know. Other times when it did make sense for a fleeting second or two, it only came out in verse. Needless to say, I felt increasingly bewildered by the changes in my emotions that happened while I was there. I was feeling deeply about things that I had no precedent for and tears would flow without really knowing why. The only thing certain was that whatever was happening in my heart was liberating and exhilarating and magical.

I wouldn't quite say that I found a home in Amritapuri or in India, itself. It was never that type of feeling of security, comfort or permanence. It was more that Amritapuri found a home in me. After three years I knew that something in me was no longer mine. Regardless of where I was to go, I knew that a part of my heart, a mysterious part, belonged to Amritapuri and even to India. My heart had revealed itself as a place of many rooms, some I had not ever been in before, and quite a few of those rooms were owned by others, where I might go, but only as a visitor. Some of these rooms included activities, feelings and even languages of which I was unaware. And still am unaware.

One thing that Amritapuri left me with is a sense of the permanent mystery of the Divine. My love for that place is a part of that mystery and that's why I can say that a part of me will always reside there. Any place where such vital and treasured memories are created sign a permanent lease within the heart. And thankfully, there is no eviction clause.

Love is in My Mother,
the Moon

ONE

Dearest One, Blessed One,
Beloved,
Bring me, Oh Please
towards You now!
Grab me fiercely with just one
Of your thousand red-palmed hands--
I wait, and every moment
before you come
Is like trash in the street.

You have been so gentle with me.
Never shocking me with surprise,
loud noises or jolting motion.
Instead, you send out a low pitch or the sound of chanting
to signal your coming.
But I am all grown up now
{Or so I pretend}
and am ready to meet you
Around unknown corners.

Isn't this why I play this game?
Of hide and seek, of separation, pain of separation and
Exquisite joy of the pain of separation?
I don't think I am the only
Actor on this stage--so

Please!
The time is now
to throw the peanuts,
To pull the cord.

Drop that bucket held way up high,
which will Only drench me completely.
The audience will shriek with laughter
No doubt!
but I too, will be laughing inside.
A laughter with my tongue out around.

In that moment--
seeing past my eyes,
Past time and space--to our eternal Union.

TWO

Sitting at the feet of God.
How awful!
There is this and there is that.
And there is a problem with this and a problem with that.
How for a moment could I think that this
could bring lasting contentment?
Is it not really just sad and confused?
Really needing the Herculean Love and compassion
that only a truly empty mind
can give.

THREE

Death princess!
Swear by me!
I look to you only.

When I was born I had your spoon in my mouth!
Your marks,
Dark islands of night,
are all over my body!
Midnight you come
and mid-winter I too
Am there!

Acknowledge me now, your eternal lover!
Bring me back from the orphanage of samsara.[1]
I see only sorrow here!

Everything shakes with an unsettling shimmering.
I am queasy from the smells of my Mind.
Soft corners with clear air
Are hard to find!

So Please,
Come back to me
And never leave again!

FOUR

My breath
starts from a place
beyond my body,
Flows through this tube of flesh,
cooling the nerves
To return to the quiet still
Peaceful Source.
I breathe like this somehow,
as a dentist pulls teeth from the mouth,
as leeches draw blood from the shin,
as sounds crack the bones of the inner ear,
as sunlight burns out the retina of the dilated eye,
as the body hair rots, leaving itchy swollen skin behind,
as the mind is tortured by a thousand conflicting thoughts,
scattered over the past, present and future,
as salty water crashes over the head, entering the nose and
clogging the lungs.

This SHIP is going down!
in and out—
the breath continues nonetheless,
like a chain of steel links,
ends bound,
In one continuous loop.

FIVE

There is no perception of any worth what-SO-ever.
Any knowledge coming through the senses is like
picking up dirty bricks
along a long walk.

In the heart of hearts
there is an open field
of which the horizon cannot be gauged--
in which the mind loses its center--
within which there is an unlimited amount of true knowing--
that quenches all desires
in even the smallest quantities.

Dive in! --
Even a toe managing to enter there
is enough Peace
For an army of elephants.

SIX

So glorious!
So glorious!
Standing up
Beyond the mind!
In all things!
Double woman--
Justice & strength.
6 eyed woman--
Grace, faith, humility.
Who reaches not
and yet,
whose hand is on every shoulder.
Look my way!
Lead me alone to the sole red sun,
burning passion,
Heart of the universe:
(Humming, burning beyond contact),
Absolute truth of the turning wheel and of this fleeting
world,
Take me nowhere!
Lead me nowhere!
(because I am eternally content to remain at your feet.)
Only keep a hand on me so that I never turn away
and get lost in that
Infinitely spitting mist
that makes up EVERY moment
Ignorant of your beauty.

SEVEN

Brahmin Kite[2]
Coast this way!
Give me shelter
of the shadow beneath your wings.
Your red earth body, capped
with your snow white head and neck
symbolizes the ultimate state
and brings the earth and the ocean
together in a siva shakti union.[3]
Your eerie call reaches the dead
across the great expanses of planes,
bringing a whole life down
to the span of a day,
of an hour,
of a moment.

EIGHT

Whoa! Sand through the fingers
goes the soul!
As prakriti[4] does her work
to reveal the strings
behind "my" oooh-so treasured story.
What once was gold,

the pride of kings,
A symbol of hope for the future--
turns out to be worthless.
Just a thin shell with moldy cheese inside!

So goes my soul,
the journey of "me:"
From violent, angry egomaniac
to knower of the Self--
Blessing to the family, to the land—
And now . . .?

nothing but a pile of bingo chips
stacked in a certain way
and leaning against a slanting wall.
What Is That?

Is it worth even a second's glance?
Much less, the reverence given towards a Micheangelo marble
statue?

Oh, wind-carved phallic pillar of rock!
Why, oh why, do I stand guard By you?
Posing Here, as if you are mine, the work of my hand?
Why, oh why, do I fret over this body, this vehicle for
consciousness,
this flash in the pan
Of the Divine Mind?

I see the pattern
I see the script
The drama all forecast in advance,
The play between mother and son--

The fears of rejection, the desire to be needed,
That desire thwarted, only
to lead to letting go
again and again.
WHO can be blamed?

towards WHO can anger be expressed?
Either way--
the story moves steadily ever towards
Relinquishment.

But each time, that step forward
is just added--
like a feather in the cap-- to the soul!
Argghhh.

"I" truly AM nothing!
Without any power
to become anything ELSE!
For how can a fictional character in a movie ever step off the
screen? . . .
no matter What
training, practice, knowledge, insight, virtue is gained?
And So,
Self-power,
I must say good-bye to you!

Even if you were viable any more,
Towards what would I engage you?
What could I ever honestly desire to change?
Knowing now
that all changes are ALWAYS already
in the script.

19

NINE

Choose Love
Forgiveness
Compassion
Generosity
Patience
Gentleness
Silence
Acceptance
Stoicism
Contentment
Optimism
Sweetness!
Because any other choice is a circle
That goes nowhere.

TEN

To Love Blindly, Impossibly, Is
To Be free.
To Celebrate one's own death
    one's own
    Decay
    Failure
    Stoppage
    Seizure
    Cessation
    Collapse
    Stillness
    Burning
Now and then,
Without reason.
Because even death cannot deliver
    A reason
    To consider,
    To weigh,
    To assess,
    To feel,
    Real loss or gain.

ELEVEN

Apple mountain Mother!
Your sweetness glows throughout the universe
leading everything with a soft soothing glare.
I feel as if I could feed forever
within the swath of its light.

It calls out to the blood flowing through my heart,
"Come to me! Come home, my darling!"

"Trouble yourself no longer
over the question of whether there is Love in the Universe!"

"Rise Up and Love, for you are me and I am You!
My victory is Yours, to sing,
To celebrate, to breathe,
to Dance
Through
Forever!"

TWELVE

You'll never encounter
A better reason to Love,
to simply Love,
Than the one you have now,
because you have None now
and that will never change.

So choose Love now
and disregard all worries and complaints,
for They multiply like rabbits
when fed the food of attention.

But peace expands like a balloon
when Objectless Joy is forced into the otherwise
worthless mind.
And if held there,
it grows like moss
over a tropical shady rock--
Taking over and covering All.

And then--
no matter what happens,
You will always have a soft place to sit and
Wait out a storm.

THIRTEEN

No longer do I need to stay slim
Loose, agile, strong, disciplined,
controlled and ready
for the next possible onslaught of infinity,
for the next random persecution of matter,
Knowing now that love and infinity are never separate,
Never at odds,
Knowing that vulnerability is the divinely intended condition,
that sickness and lack are God-given cures to counteract
only way more insidious painful internal conditions--
Like ignorance of Him produced by addictions to the pain of
diversity.

But now I have taken all the pills,
my eyes are forever cleared,
knowing truth that is beyond the mind,
Knowing without doubt that the world of the senses is merely
a cloud-- dressing the Earth with shadows,
covering the ever present Sun.

A new page has been turned.
A new story of trust being told—
Trust,
based in some type of knowing,
that I am always PRE-"seen."

My love for truth acknowledged,
a divine love now rains down

washing away Kali's[5] unpredictable wrath,
cleansing even the approach of death,
leaving only the residue
of the never-ending Divine caress.

FOURTEEN

"What?!?
Am I not allowed this?"
Red bindu[6] blood flows freely.
If Mother Earth owns this body
and the steps upon which it stumbles,
Can anything be said to have happened?

Madhura![7]
Sweetness!
If there is such a thing as Me,
then it IS this cry
in response to my Mother's body.
Madhura! Sweetness!
This world! This life!
This attitude! Objectless Love!

FIFTEEN

How long?
How long till the Ego takes over again?
How long?
Till the stupor returns?
Till the "I" falls back asleep?
After clinging once again--
re-charged with making something of "Kilaya,"
Passionate all over again for "my" own cause--
Trying to rejoin my Mother,
Or some other nonsense!
Always
partial to "these" conditions over "those."

I thought that I was drowning,
I thought that I was burning,
But it is much worse that that--
This whole life story is a lie whether it's on fire or not,
A misery-making machine!
A machine
whose own arm is stuck within its own gears--
And so,
This machine does not work properly and can't be fixed!

Leave it by the side of the road, man!
Why are you dragging it behind you?
Like a mule carrying its cruel masters' bundles?
It weighs you down/ constricts your throat
And keeps you from either dancing or singing. . . .

SIXTEEN

It's all over man!
your make-up has smeared
and your wig has fallen to the floor
leaving a horrible crater exposed.
Seeing That in the mirror,
the mind stops
with nothing to champion,
nothing to promote,
no substance to work with,
no clay to mold,
no wood to carve.

What happens in the shop
when all the tools are sharp & fully charged
but there is not a speck of wood
to work with?
How long will you go on pretending?
drunk with memories,
deluded by emotions,
going through the motions
that you still have a job,
that you're still doing something,
crafting something,
shifting something,
in this world?

Not knowing what else to do,
you keep doing,
and prop up the backdrop to keep that story
believable.
But now the phone has rang
and then rings again,

calling you away once again
from your deluded play.

and reminding you of what you have been trying not to know
that it is time to let it go
and come home.

SEVENTEEN

Who am I to Love You, my Lord?
Who am I to Love You, my Lady?
I am nothing but effort:
going through the motions,
of doing things,
putting things together,
trying to express a thought.
But nothing comes through, nothing
comes out
without your doing.
You achieve the results of my
fumbling awkward attempts.
In this way, how can I prove my love?
how can I act out my love?
how can I even express my love for you
without you bringing it through?
without you there to turn an intention,
an orientation, an inherent Nature
into an expression, a manifestation?

EIGHTEEN

I have the keys to the kingdom of peace now,
but they are worthless in the absence of an individual self.
Why would you water dunes of the desert?
Millions of gallons of water can be poured out
and a minute later not a single puddle will remain--
And certainly nothing green will ever grow!
For this reason, I can Now not even approach my Mother.
What she gives
In what bucket
Do I put it?

NINETEEN

The process is not about becoming LibeRated--
but rather about letting go of what is bound
in favor of what is already free.
For, how can a prison cell be set free?
How can steel bars be released?

After countless lifetimes
This cell-
This body and mind-
Are ALL I know . . .
And so, OF COURSE--

I keep trying to drag it out the window.
And I am endlessly frustrated
when it refuses to budge.

Oh, changing sands of time--
Cease your pretense Of any importance!
You block the glorious colors of the forever-setting Sun!

TWENTY

Call me jack,
the pirate slave trader
who bound and gagged me
a long time ago
in a foreign land,
Stowed me below deck in a dark and dank corner of a ship
where I was tossed around
like a dirty plastic bottle
by the slaps of crashing waves.
And now I walk with shaky legs in this strange world,
still flinching at the sound of footsteps,
not quite sure how and why I got free
and what to do
with the bewilderment,
the frustration, anger and detachment,
not to mention the startling fact
that this new land
Resembles so subtly
the paradise of my dreams.

TWENTY-ONE

Deep within the cave of the Goddess
Eternal secrets are revealed.
I now see Devi[8] everywhere.
She is in everyone in disguise to herself.
in every form
She looks at me with intensity,
just as a woman looks at herself in a mirror.
She's at play and she's deadly serious about it.
I must play along—
For how can she play
if she knows it's only her?
"Don't ruin my fun" she says
to herself,
"And I'll let you in on the game—"
wink, wink,
"And then, you will no longer think that anything is ever lost
Or gained . . ."

TWENTY-TWO

This body, mind, this
story, this "I"
is the theatre
where They come
just for me
to set me free,
To bring me home.

TWENTY-THREE

Living Whole, Being Full, Complete
Is a simple but comprehensive acceptance
of the facts,
both obvious and subtle,
of right now,
without any ideas of understanding,
judgment of consequence,
cause or effect, significance, meaning
or even relevance to Divine Beneficent Truth

or contact with Me.
That is Liberation.
Open eyes,
accepting everything,
seeing nothing
of Note.

TWENTY-FOUR

God is my asset--
God is my sole possession--
In God's hands I rest.
Turning away from the fleeting nature of the joy given by
anything else,
I release myself to Her.

TWENTY-FIVE

Unattached attention
without judgement, free,
without weight, without caution,
like light shinning into a nighttime jungle scene,
warm and assured
Is Param Prema, Supreme Love.

TWENTY-SIX

Oneness is like a telescope--
Through one end,
Zoom in and
You're looking at the world.
And through the other--
the world is looking at you.
Are they really different?
Near or far,
highlighted or obscured,
what IS
is still the same, either way.

TWENTY-SEVEN

With this feeling, it is undone that which needs to be undone.
 With this sight it is undone that which needs to be undone.
 With this sound it is undone that which needs to be undone.
 With this smell it is undone that which needs to be undone.
 With this idea it is undone that which needs to be undone.

TWENTY-EIGHT

Oh, Mother vision vine!
Where are you now?
How could we have been so close?
How could you have showed
Yourself to me
for Just a fleeting moment?
revealing all,
Answering all,
Rooting out doubt,
and now, You're gone!
Where are You?
Please tell me where to go--
what to do?
To see you again!
and Stay this time.

TWENTY-NINE

This Body--!
It is my duty to abandon You!
Do not worry!
You are in much better
hands now!
Just remember--
Continue to breathe!
through that straw
that is eternally connected
to the fresh cool mountain air.
Keep your head
always above the waves
and take in the soothing soft caress
of the saline womb water
down below.

THIRTY

In action, actor and object acted upon, there is only Ishwara.[9]

Apart from that, there is attitude towards Ishwara or
Attitude towards THIS.
Love injects attention and scrutiny into the attitude towards
THIS,
building until Ishwara alone is seen.

THIRTY-ONE

This story pushes me
Around.
Is that valid?
There's nothing to it
No mystery x--
No unknown
To solve for--
To worry about.

THIRTY-TWO

When I say IMPOSSIBLE!
I mean
Taken as a whole--
Without a single redeemable quality--
Without a single cause for joy--
Except its emptiness.

This present moment
Is about as attractive
To pick up and possess
As a turd in the street.

THIRTY-THREE

How DOES a movie intrigue?
I need to know.
Is it imagining that we are there?
Involved with tom cruise
Working with meryl streep?
a king's magician
Or a wealthy manhattan power broker?
Or just an average person
living a mysterious but normal life?
What about it
gives the mind pleasure?
Is it the open ended nature—
that anything can happen
(or can appear to happen?)
combined with the fact that nothing at all
is ever really happening?

IS IT the fact that I truly feel involved,
that something really hinges on my efforts,
that keeps me from really sitting back,
Laughing/delighting in it all
and munching on popcorn.

How does a movie NOT intrigue?
No matter what the content.

THIRTY-FOUR

How can I possibly take this
body, these lips, these hands,
this mind, these thoughts, this
understanding
and make an offering to what is
beyond –?
to what is perfect,
to what needs no light,
to what needs no support,
to what sees neither lack nor
fullness?

You are beyond
all reckoning,
all limitations of absorbability,
all comparison,
all ascribing,
all assessing,
all contact,
all thought.
In this light,
What is my sadhana?[10]
What are my efforts,
my remembrances,
my diligences in practice,
my mouthings of words,
repeating the words of others,
who too,
have seen you,

and for lack of an answer,
have done Something ---
anything, in Response.

Bow down, paint one's forehead, avert
one's eyes, make ablutions,
abhisekkas, circumambulations,[11]
certain styles of dress, times
of eating, vows, recitations,
recordations. . . .

All in an effort to approach, to
bring down and to raise up,
so
that what is here can reach
what is there:
I follow
the Wisdom of the sages, instructions
passed down through the ages
and received as a gift
through eons of accumulated merit.

But is this all Not now to be seen
as the ultimate abode of pride?
of the ego, of some essential
substance that "I am"?
somewhere in which I try to abide, to which the ego clings?

If I have reached a door where
I can see You and
no longer pretend any contact —
any similarity —
any resemblance —
between Your characteristics and mine,

Can I continue to pretend to Be
standing upright any longer?
on my own?
with some value?
NO.
Knowing the difference between
You and I
I am delivered.

Freed to go where I go,
without judgement,
without difference,
You go there —nowhere, everywhere,
effective always, good forever, the Savior.
I go here — to death, to an end,
helpless,
powerless till the end,
the Saved,
the Redeemed,
I LOVE YOU!
NOT ME!
I love that which is Love,
infinite love, perfect Love,
the undeniably lovable!

You
Love All Things!
Even the unlovable,
the false, the pathetic.
Are We Not two sides of the Same coin?
Why would the tail of the coin
want to be the head?

Cannot the tail rest in being the
tail? . . .
knowing there is always a
head nearby?
Why would the tail worry, think
or try to Become the head?

And if, by some miracle someday,
this happens and the tail is the head
then it will only be through a contentment
with the differences —
that comes from seeing and feeling
and resting in the Sameness.

My Idea of sadhana is done.
Seen now as the last crutch
of discontentment and wishing for change.

THIRTY-FIVE

I'm throwing my life out the window.
Kicking it, like an old dog, out of my bed,
where it has been leaving fleas and bed bugs,
Farting and tracking in mud.
I don't want to be an old man reminiscing
Near a fire
Sighing, bitter-sweetly,
over a mysteriously full life,
valuing my relationship to God,
Full of wisdom, self-satisfaction
And love.
As if I had done okay
Given the size of the difficulties.
Having fought many battles and somehow having won even
those I lost.

No, Rather
I'd prefer to live right now
As one already dead,
Blank and non-existent,
Noticing the container-like world
with all its colors and
Its own eyes to see them
And its own hand
To pen this poem.

THIRTY-SIX

The choice of consciousness:
--looking at the whole from the eye
--looking at the eye from the whole

THIRTY-SEVEN

Phantom work,
Sector 5!
Take your phantom gear
And your phantom views--
Don't worry!
A soft touch on their phantom cheeks
Always works--
although the seasoned vets have moved on
to a more efficient
Raspy roar--which is
Certain to move back a crowd
of phantom dullards and insurgents.
Of course,
Training for the roar requires a Degree
in small self annihilation.

THIRTY-EIGHT

Deadly are these days!
Chained to the illusory self!
Oppressed by universal madness
Closed off to the roads of success--
Save ME please,
O Mother of the world!
Pick me up and set me on my feet--
Facing eternity, and with enough speed
to sit back and relax
(Within my own shell),
Knowing a crash
(a Crash!)
Is the destination,
Blood – the prize.

THIRTY-NINE

"Good news!" you say emphatically.
"Good news!" you say again!
What is "Good?"
Everything I see is unsatisfactory in my sight!
"Good" is that place
A pace away
From good and bad.
Sit there and you will hear it yourself,
That's "Good" News!

FORTY

You!
Who have valued the mind so much!
You're just playing with ideas!
And when you play with ideas
with what are you playing?

Can you build anything of substance with ideas?
If you add up 2 ideas can you get something you can call 3?
This "Love"
Is it not, too,
a sham?

a short-changed life?
No substitute for clear vision RIGHT now,
Seeing the difference and the interplay between truth and
fiction,
Between the impermanent and the eternal.

FORTY-ONE

This body IS insensate!
For how can a nose smell a nose?
Or an eye see itself?
Or a fingertip know of the roughness of its own skin?
the body
and that which it senses
Are not two!
So where are those feelings coming from?
COULD
they just be ideas?
In the cosmic mind?
Engaged by choice and habit of choice
Alone?

FORTY-TWO

You're running around today,
my center of joy,
going to play with the others,
leaving me alone
and empty.
Can't I just say that you are there?
whether you are
here or not?

FORTY-THREE

Anchored in the good feeling
of uninhibited Being,
dwelling in the threat of death
inherent in our social
relations,
A Still Mind flows,
holding the blackmail
of the Breath at Bay
by keeping it always
front and center,
clear
within an unblinking
and undistracted eye.

FORTY-FOUR

She decides what's
On stage today.
If you don't like it
That's Her too.

FORTY-FIVE

Who is thinking this thought?!?
How do YOU feel about the
      process of contracting and
      then expanding into Stillness?
Do you see it as an attack
      or as a love-making?
With what attitude do YOU
      approach your next dental
      appointment?
Dreading the whole affair? or
      blissed out over the thought
      of a clean and healthy
      mouth?

FORTY-SIX

You talk about the anguish of forgetting the greatness of the
                    Lord . . .?
What about the anguish of forgetting the vacancy of the self?
That heart-wrenching despair in the realization that you have
                    once again
            Put all your money
      in the pocket with the hole in it!
                    And so,
            are flat broke,
      back to zero again.

FORTY-SEVEN

It always comes back to this:
"I see it As It Is now and so,
Why aren't I being treated differently?"
Ha Ha Ha!
The ego will even become God in order to win over the
world.
And so, I sit, thinking--
And am sunk.
For does not even the deferral of my actions to God require
some process of thought?
If there is a crossroads where I do not follow impulse without
significance

FORTY-EIGHT

My body is also Amma,
    another disguise of the guru,
    to which I bow down
    and lower my head
As a dog greets its master
    with a wagging tail
    and lowered eyes.
For what other form
    appears there before it?
    greeting me in the morning,
    in front of me always,
    waiting to guide me,
    in the end,
through the final door.

FORTY-NINE

Surrendered to You
I am Too Tired to
    Remember a Thing.
I am naked
    without even my own jewels.
I disregard the gunas[12]--
    even my name,
I sometimes cannot remember.

You are filling in my gap
and I am losing my center,
Which is that place
in which
I have stored myself
for SO many generations.

FIFTY

You're here,
You will always be right here,
like the white-washed brick wall
upon which this movie is showing.
YOU will remain
even when the lights go out.

The details are just a play,
just for fun,
just for love,
an unimaginable impossible Love,
unreachable,
inexpressible
for anyone but God!
but You!

FIFTY-ONE

All that happiness,
all that pain and suffering,
every instance of contraction,
of squeezing
Can either be given new life by engagement
Or it can be deflated
by non reaction.

Remember, Muni,[13]
Remember!

Every pain is an open
door to Remember Love
and bask in the True Self
That is Beyond the
limited and otherwise
Meaningless Image in
the Mirror.

Break the Mirror!
Remember, Remember!

FIFTY-TWO

Whose Charade is this?
Why does this story enchant
    you so much?
Why do you turn it over
    in the light of the night
    like a precious gem
    in a rich man's sweaty hand?
Why are you proud of what has
    come?
Why are you excited by the
    possible future permutations
    of all the new potential additions?
Do you think someday the
    stack will be so tall, so deep
    and so grand
that you will take it with you?
That someday you will
    finally say "See! . . How
    great It is! Permanent!
    . . . now . . . It is forever Me!"?

How can you forget what you
    once so Clearly saw?
When you looked deeply into your sack,
    your story,
    and saw the gaping hole
    down below.

All this will be gone, fool!
    Forgotten,
    nothing, dust, SHINING dust
in the wind . . .
    Fodder for rodents,
    food for flies.
All of this,
which you are so ready to defend,
    Gone!

To Whom are you trying to Prove
    your greatness?
Who is it that holds on to
    this story as valuable?
Who is it that interacts
    with others competitively, saying
    This is Mine/Me,
That is Yours, You?

FIFTY-THREE

I am Your Only Devotee
Throughout the Entire
Universe I see No one
Who loves You
Like I do.

Accept my love now!
Let's Drop the Charade,
Stop the Pretending,
that we are in a crowd,
in public,
No! It's Not True!
There's no one between You and me!

except these eyes
and these words.

FIFTY-FOUR

In Loving the only thing I risk
    is being a fool
    is being wrong
    is being mean
    is acting improperly,
    is releasing a demon.
In giving service
    weariness may come,
    short-temper,
    short-sightedness,
    superficial gossiping,
    slanderous speech also.
But none of it could ever be carried forward
    to tarnish who I am.
Why preserve/create a good reputation
    instead of honoring the True Self?

FIFTY-FIVE

This moment may be yours.
In fact, Every moment is yours.
But
Love is Mine,
Love is Me,
Outside of Here and Now
(and THAT I am happy to let go of!)

[Holding onto the Here and Now
is like a dog barking
at its own reflection in a puddle
or like a man trying
to shave the beard
that he sees
on the face
in the mirror.]

FIFTY-SIX

I exist is not the
    underlying basis of reality.
I love and am loved is.

FIFTY-SEVEN

YOU ARE BEING BOWLED OVER
but it is only resistance that is
a problem.

TURN AROUND,
right now
and swim with the river.

NOT A SINGLE OTHER PERSON
is involved.

THERE IS NO ONE IN THIS UNIVERSE
other than
your decision to love. Right now.

FIFTY-EIGHT

Life is Like Riding a Mechanical Bull.
it's a rough ride
going nowhere.
The only Victory is in
the End when one
can rest.

FIFTY-NINE

Stillness is golden,
Stillness is profound,
Nothing stopped in any way.
Everything alive, shining
from within.
A fullness that requires
nothing and
shimmers in step with
all diversity.
Rainbow hued, rich and safe,
withdrawn from all
self-propulsion.
Careening through space
while the stars and planets
shine.
Loving Impossibly
Impossible Love!
It takes two to
complete an impossible
love.
Me alone, forever, I
look to you
in Love.
Falling short because
I have no where to stand
and have nothing to see
you with!
I am
Needing you Now
to complete this Love!
Needing you Now to make
an impossible Love
True, here and now!

SIXTY

I can't know anything!
I am silly, naïve,
    innocent, foolish,
    call it what you want.
I need a partner, a friend,
    who has clear eyes,
    isn't always smiling,
who can wade through the
    swampy reeds for me,
clear the hidden
    glass shards and mark
    the sharp rocks,
    sturdy the raft,
    or pick up the breeze.
Leaving me free to breathe
    and smile, fearless,
    blind as a bat,
    in Love.

SIXTY-ONE

Seeing bunnies on the lawn
Come together, hop away.

SIXTY-TWO

Why should life work out
for something that is
insubstantial?
Why should it All be for
something that has no Core,
no true Content?
Why would you place
precious eggs
into a cracked unfired
mud bowl?
This is the essence of
Renunciation.

Life is geared for the only
thing that is substantial,
the only thing that can hold
onto the profits of hard
work,
the only thing that will
reliably last throughout
all the changing conditions
of time and space.
"I" am nothing but a
fleeting but substantial
remembering,
recognition, celebration
and so, Creator of that fact.

In remembering, I recognize the truth.
In recognizing, I can

celebrate, in celebrating
I can create
and in creating
I am none other than
what I create – that
Eternal Truth of
Wholeness, Fullness, Love,
Bliss, Power.

Drop the Charade!
Get going on this Right now!

SIXTY-THREE

Looking from within it is pain.
Looking from without it is God's
    glory.
Looking from everywhere and nowhere
    at once
    all is silence, stillness
    peace.
Come to me in silence, stillness!
    we will work it out,
    where all is already done.
And now, knowing that,
    let's sing and dance together
    free of worries,
    free of thought.

SIXTY-FOUR

Pain is Play.
Pain is the Stage
upon which Love Dances.
One Taste to all Things.
    No success.
    No Failure.
I give life to all things
    by setting them free.
The seed emerges from
    my body mind
And takes a trip all of its own.
Clearly not me & yet
    the apple of my heart!
Sometimes I follow after it –
    raising a hand—
But then I remember Love,
    and back off
    with a quivering sigh.

SIXTY-FIVE

Mind is Anguish
Body is Pain
Time is Pressure

SIXTY-SIX

Walk this way
through the crease of life
on the way to freedom.
I met it halfway,
knowing the deal was rigged.

Within me I was carrying
what I was running from
and I cried silent tears
to think that someday
it might catch up to others.

In the midst of such fears
it was hiding,
working me over,
and pretending no harm,
not having touched
even one other soul.

Now I lie with this man
and his quick fingers--
which now, only reach
for others' throats.

SIXTY-SEVEN

I suffer the experience
    of only one,
    of infinite variety,
    of unpredictable nature and outcome,
    of uncontrollable results.

Because I am Love,
    I am One,
    I am Beyond
        all words, all thoughts,
        all experience.

I suffer because I cannot be touched
    and so, allow all things,
    as a testament to my
    indescribable
    non demonstrable greatness.

SIXTY-EIGHT

Revulsion swallows me whole
    when the extent of Maya[14] is revealed.
Who is revolted?
Even this question churns the stomach and
    breaks down the nerves.
How could I ever
    celebrate something of this world,
    ever?
Knowing that everything is fleeting, everything
    a "lie?"
How could I get caught up,
    like flotsam snagged
    on the bow of a ship,
in another's leg-kicking antics?
    /amusements?
    /fascinations?
    /possibilities?
    /plans?
    /hopes?
    /enthusiasms?
Where does it all go,
    this dust-devil of parts,
    if everything is already
    still like a star?

SIXTY-NINE

A phenomena cannot be liberated.
With the body goes the mind,
the memory, the stance, the location,
the objectives, the needs, the viewpoint,
the problems.

SEVENTY

From a fear of death
the value of life arises.
From the value of life
the desire to build arises,
    to make one's mark,
    to hold off death,
    to express love & hope.
Holding off death, busyness emerges,
    along with the struggle to awaken
    and stay awake.

Sleep is a fog overcoming consciousness.
to fight it we engage in all sorts of activity
    propping up interest, desires, lust
    even anxiety
    artificially.
so that we may feel more alive than dead.

Rip Van Winkle fell asleep for 3 years.
It could have been a 3 year meditation,
    dead to the world and
    re-emerging without care:
Care to live,
    care to cause others to live,
    invested in this or any story. . .

It is natural to hold on possessively
    to consciousness,
But where am I going with this idea
    and my struggle with this idea?

How long will I be willing to be artificial, to
be FAKE,
    just to be a section in a future
    "Lives of the Yogis" compilation?

For how much longer will I resist the
absolute stillness,
    silence,
    that is at least half of life,
    that breaks down all ideas,
    yielding an effortless, joyous life
    that flows like water,
    unconcerned with the size and direction
of the ditch
    in which it travels?

For how much longer will I stay up
    to write this poetry?

SEVENTY-ONE

She doesn't need to move,
    to enjoy the "I AM:"
the Dream of Existence,
Vátsalayai.[15]

I am all One.
A single Love
directed towards
    What is Not Real or Unreal
    but What
    is Wholeness.
And Seeing All Movements,
    All thoughts,
    all Differentiation,
    all Diversity,
    all Judgement,
    all Fear,
as powerless to Touch
    or affect the Single Truth
of Goodwill and Magnanimity.

SEVENTY-TWO

What can I control
        and what can I not
control right now:
is the essence of discrimination.

Staying in control
        of what is controllable and
        not interfering with
what is not:
is the essence of Love.

Do not attempt to control
        or inhibit what is
        given,
what is already there
        in each moment.

Instead,
guide it like you would a child,
        taking bity steps forward,
        into the beyond.

SEVENTY-THREE

Have I laughed today, you ask?
   I AM THE ONLY ONE
   HERE. . . !
what is painful,
what is revolting,
what is disgusting,
what is just plain wrong,
   stupid,
   not good,
   foolish,
   cruel,
   unnecessary,
is just an event of objects that has been created by me
   for transcendence—
as a door back
   to truth—
   back to joy—
   back to freedom—
   back to love—of the whole—
   back to my own all-inclusive infinite nature!

Yes, I have laughed today,
   with tears flying out around.

SEVENTY-FOUR

She plays with nothing but
    loss.
Her bliss is built upon
    pain, frustration and confusion.
Face your music,
    then and only then,
    can you stand in Her fire,
    in Her bliss
    and not get burnt.
Try to pick it up,
    stand in Her shoes and
    transcend the pain . . .Ha!
you're done for,
    cooked—
    doomed to cry once again.

SEVENTY-FIVE

One taste:
the emotions are like red-hot flowing lava:
    beautiful from afar,
    leaving a scorched mark behind,
    having a bright red tip
    that quickly turns black with soot.

The senses are like sharp knives:
    gleaming bright as they flash around,
    leaving cuts and punctures
    that soon bleed.

Social interactions are like nuclear power:
    intensely hot and
    cooking you from the inside out.

Time is like having your skin pulled from your body
    by a fish-hook tied to a tree.
Thoughts are like swallowing poison
    mixed with small glass shards
    that cut again
    on the way back up.

Phenomenal World! I see you!

SEVENTY-SIX

And I dance on the carnage of Your body!
Chinnamasta![16]
I hold Your head in my hands
    and kiss Your blood-caked lips!
O Mother!
I see all these bodies
    bleeding and burning.
Why are they walking around
    smiling without any teeth?

SEVENTY-SEVEN

The drag that you feel is the platform that She dances on,
    in celebration of You.
    Recognize what's what!
I want 38 lifetimes
    appreciating this!
I am born to my inherent Love for You,
    She says.
I have given Her the time and space
    in order to stand apart from Me.
And I have forgotten what I have done
    so that She can pretend to search for,
    to find Me and then
    celebrate Me.
the price I have paid is an eternity of suffering
    in the fog of forgetfulness and
    in the ignorance of confusion.

SEVENTY-EIGHT

Not just the ego but
everything will be dissolved
when the separate "I" ceases and
Home, Wholeness, shines again.

So it's not just your return!
But, everyone and everything's!
The stage screens come down,

the props are put away
and the actors go home
when the show wraps.

When the potter's wheel stops spinning and
the pot removed,
all the clay is cleaned up,
even what has dried and
fallen to the floor.

SEVENTY-NINE

What Is —
Is the Divine surf board
Upon which you ride the Divine Waves of Bliss,
No mind necessary.

EIGHTY

Loss with no recourse
is the Tao, is the presence of God,
is my heart full of love.
It is available in every moment, an ocean
to jump into and swim around in, death itself,
the ultimate and everyman's merging with Absolute Truth,
Absolute consciousness, Pure Love.

How could I
hold anything back,
through this pat down with death?
only what's not possess-able
gets thru.

EIGHTY-ONE

After all these years since the Boyton Cave[17]
    when the Torrent came through,
you have yet to make the mind your enemy.

You still trust the mind in the moment of
    activity,
    of accomplishing.
You are still cooking your food
    over the photo of a flame.

You have yet to take up the sword
    of your Eternal Absolute Nature,
cutting through appearances,
seeing through your so-called "life,"
    that sham of solidity,
    that play of light,
all created by jumping shadows.

Who is it that knows this? . . .
The one who always has!
who is the source of this dream of confusion,
    of ignorance, of diversity, of isolation,
    of separation.

Why should you trouble me, O mind?
For you are NOTHING,
Nothing.

"Only You and You alone
really know Yourself
through Your own power, O great one,
Lord of all beings,
supporter of all beings,
God of the gods,
Lord of the Universe."

Arjuna speaking to Krishna,
THE BHAGAVAD GITA, verse 10:15.

NOTES

[1] SAMSARA: The condition of being forced to be born again and again, endlessly, due to ignorance and debts owed to others (karma).

[2] BRAHMIN KITE: A species of fish-eating bird common on the Kerala, India seashores where Amritapuri is located.

[3] SIVA SHAKTI UNION: The merging of the male and female aspects of the Divine.

[4] PRAKRITI: The material aspect or basis of life.

[5] KALI: The dark wrathful aspect of the Divine Mother within Hinduism.

[6] BINDHU: The mark worn on the brow between the eyebrows denoting Hindu faith.

[7] MADHURA: Literally meaning sweetness like honey.

[8] DEVI: A common name of the Divine Mother or Goddess in Hinduism.

[9] ISHWARA: An ancient name for God in India.

[10] SADHANA: A particular practice or combination of practices within Yoga undertaken for spiritual growth.

[11] ABLUTIONS, ABHISEKKAS, CIRCUMAMBULATIONS: Three common ways of showing devotion and humility within Hindu religious practice.

[12] GUNAS: The basic elements of material existence.

[13]MUNI: An epithet for a wise person or a sage.

[14]MAYA: The delusional nature of superficial or worldly life.

[15]VATSALAYAI: One of many names of the Divine Mother.

[16]CHINNAMASTA: Another aspect of the Divine Mother, this one is more wrathful, violent and gruesome than others.

[17]BOYTON CAVE: A pilgrimage site in Sedona, Arizona.

www.ingramcontent.com/pod-product-compliance
Lightning Source LLC
Chambersburg PA
CBHW021137020426
42331CB00005B/817